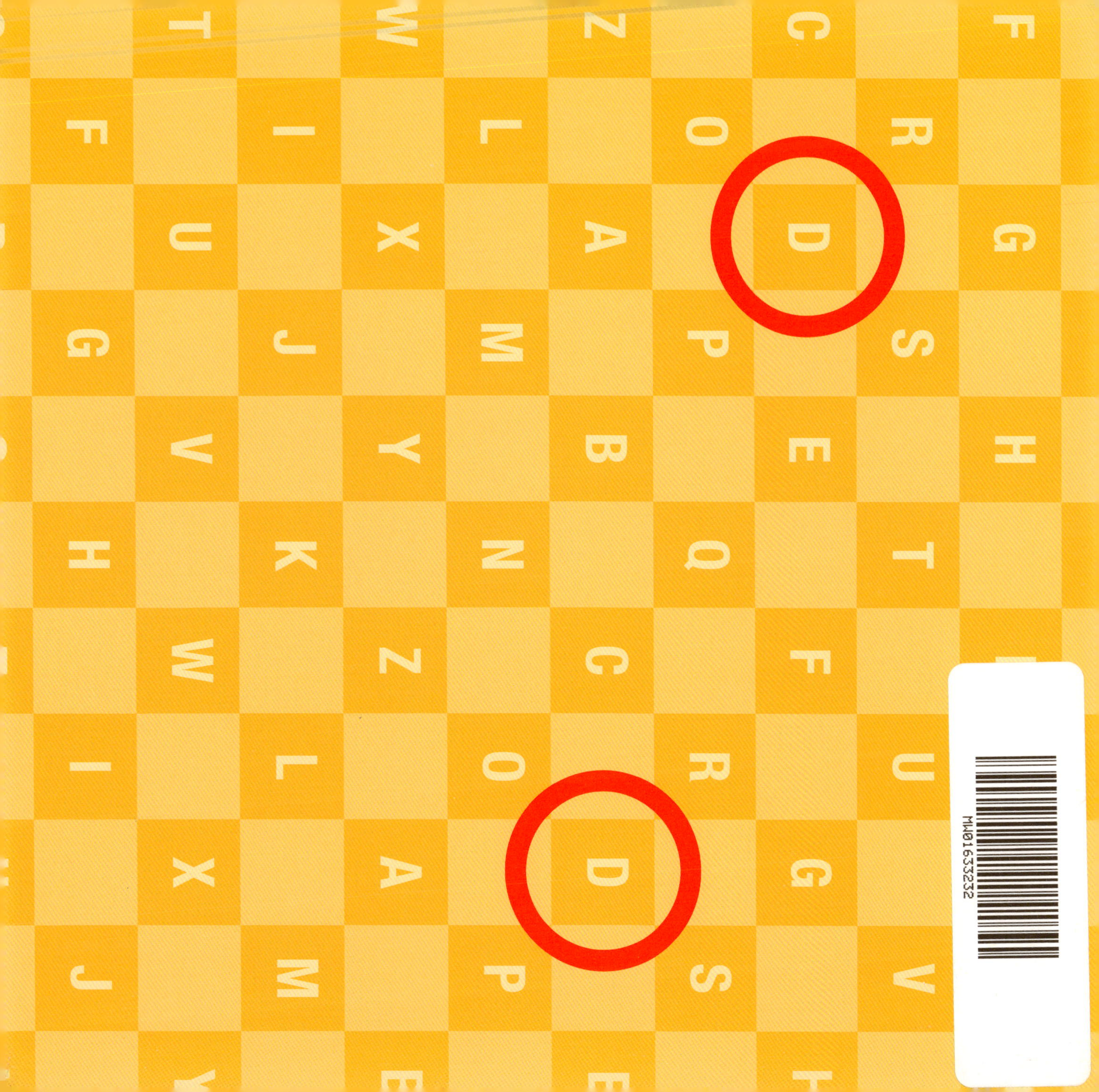

FEATURING

OUR KIDSPAK®

"D" is for DIVERSITY

by Eileen Tucker Cosby

illustrated by Norma S. Strange

www.swakpak.com

Thanks to our families and friends for believing in our mission of promoting positive lifestyles for children & their families. Their generous contributions have made it possible to make this book available to schools, churches, libraries and various community programs.

 For information regarding permission, write to SWAK Pak® LLC, 9417 S. 157th Place, Gilbert, AZ 85234, or call toll free (866) SWAK-PAK. Books and other merchandise available online at www.swakpak.com.

First Edition

ISBN 09707420-3-7
Library of Congress Cataloging-In-Publication Data Pending

OUR KIDSPAK®

JORJAK	MARISAK	RATAK	PATTIWAK
(WITH HU-JAK)	(WITH MOO-ZAK)	(WITH COZI-YAK)	(WITH YIK-YAK)

"D" is for DIVERSITY is fourth in a series featuring **Jorjak**, **Marisak**, **Ratak**, and **Pattiwak**, collectively known as **Our KidsPak**.® In this book, our lovable group of adopted characters celebrate the wonderful differences among people in the world. Race, nationality and disabilities are just a few diversity topics discussed.

Reinforcing the importance of respecting and honoring people regardless of their differences, is another way of making a positive difference in the world.

NOTE TO PARENTS: *The Our KidsPak series has been developed to promote interaction between parents and their children about various social, humanitarian, intellectual and spiritual issues. Please take time to read and discuss the content of this book with your child. The entire family will benefit from the positive messages presented.*

"D" is for **diversity.**

What does diversity mean?

It's a **celebration** of many types of people,
The most **wonderful people** you've ever seen.

RACE

Look around and what do you see?

The different **colors** of you and me.
Black, brown, white and tanned faces,
Representing the world and all the beautiful **races.**

One of the most harmful things
that you can do
Is to be unkind to **someone**
Who is a **different** color than you.

We all have a **heart.**

We all have a **brain.**

Our skin may look different,
But inside we're all **the same.**

NATIONALITY

There are many **different** places

To live in this big world;

Places with different **styles** and traditions

Celebrated by parents, boys and girls.

Many people live in Africa.

Some people live in Spain.

Maybe you were born in Japan

Or maybe you're from the Ukraine.

You could be from **here**
Or you could be from **there.**

Your nationality and
culture are **special**

And should be
respected
everywhere.

RELIGION

Each day when you take time to pray,
Children of **other faiths** are praying too.

They may not worship
And believe the way you do,

But remember **God** loves them

Just the way He **loves you.**

When you're praying,
Look to the **stars.**

Ask God to help you **love others**
Just the way they are.

DIFFERENTLY-ABLED

How do you get
from **one place**
to **another?**

Do you use your legs
or a wheelchair
like many **others?**

Do you use your ears
To **listen** to sounds far and near?
Or do you **use sign language**
Because your ears cannot hear?

None of us were born perfect.
Not **everyone** is born exactly the same.

If you know someone who is differently-abled
Treat them with **honor** and not shame.

SHAPE AND SIZE

People come in all shapes and sizes.
Some are **short** and some are **tall.**

Don't be concerned about how they measure.

But if they need you, be there when they call.

6
5
4
3
2
1

Funny Mirror

Chances are you have some **friends**
Who are **heavy** or who are **thin.**

You may have heard others make fun

Of the condition they are in.

Heavy or thin,

Short or tall;

The **size and shape** of people

Doesn't matter at all!

SOCIAL STATUS

Do not treat people harshly

Because of what they have or have not.

The **quality** of a person
Isn't **measured** by what they've got!

Anyone can be **rich**

Or have a lack of money.

It's the **kindness** in our hearts
That turns cloudy days **bright and sunny.**

OCCUPATION

In every country around the globe

There are people with different occupations.

From **building** houses to building planes,

Jobs are important to the growth of our nations.

Be grateful that people have different jobs.

Whether a scientist, an artist, or someone who drives,

Always **respect** the work done by others.

It's what helps us lead better lives.

BOYS AND GIRLS

Girls were made **special**

And so were boys.

They both have talents

And bring their parents **joy.**

Whether you're a girl

Or whether you're a boy,

You have an **equal opportunity**

To spread your wings and **soar.**

WHAT A WONDERFUL WORLD

It is wonderful to live in a world

With people of different colors, races and creeds.

A world where we can be **unique;**
A world where we can **all succeed.**

Together we can make a change,
For now and **forever** after,
To **admire** and respect our differences
And judge a person only by their **character.**

CELEBRATE
DIVERSITY!

IT'S A WONDERFUL WORLD!

I promise to respect the differences of others and judge them only by their character.

My signature reflects my dedication and promise to make this world a better place by the positive choices I make.

Date ______________________________

Grade ______________________________

Signature ____

To download a printable certificate, visit our website www.DisforDiversity.com or www.swakpak.com

Adopting a Positive Attitude.

Our KidsPak books communicate awareness of certain public issues in order to make the world a better place. Jorjak, Marisak, Ratak and Pattiwak's mission is to positively enrich the quality of life for children with their heartfelt social, humanitarian, intellectual and spiritual messages. A portion of the proceeds from all Our KidsPak books is donated to various adoption agencies, adoption foundations and adoption educational programs.

Other Our KidsPak books **AVAILABLE NOW:**

"A" is for ADOPTED

"N" is for NO SMOKING…please

"M" is for MONEY – Money Management for Kids

"D" is for DIVERSITY

"H" is for HEALTHY – Weight Management for Kids

"F" is for FAMILY

Adopting a New Way of Life.

Our KidsPak®

A Series of Positive Children's Books

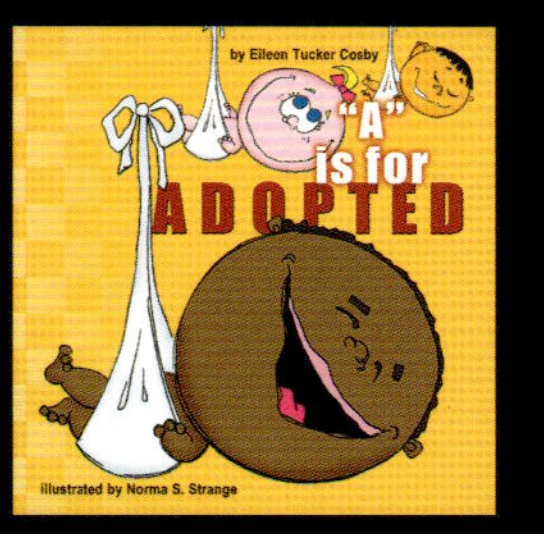

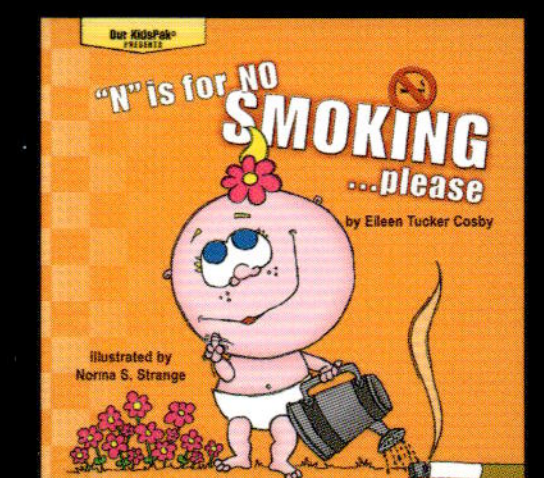

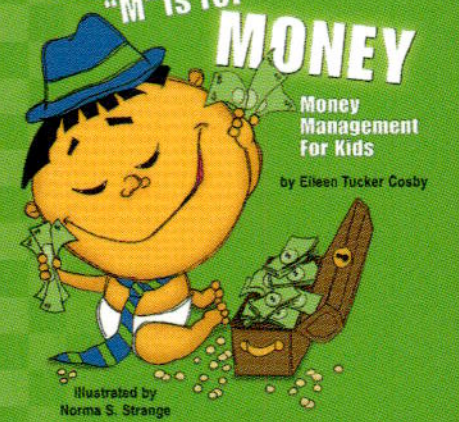

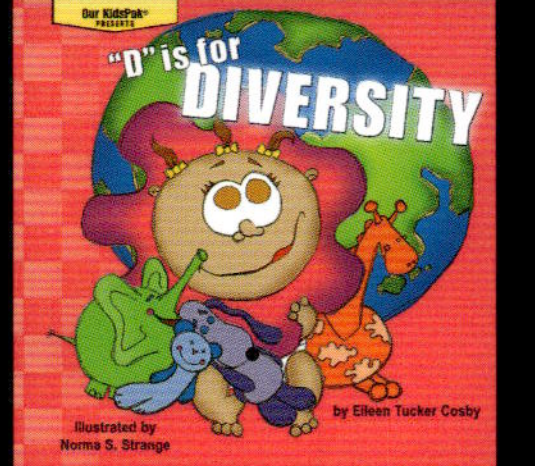

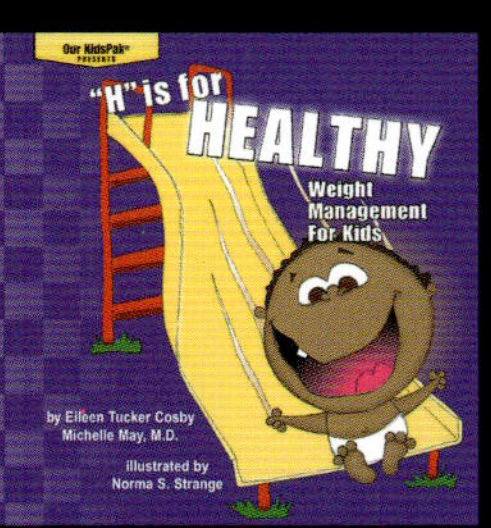

NOTE TO PARENTS: The Our KidsPak series has been developed to promote interaction between parents and their children about various social, humanitarian, intellectual and spiritual issues. Please take time to read and discuss the content of this book with your child. The entire family will benefit from the positive messages presented.

Order online, visit a major retailer or bookstore, or call for volume discount pricing.

www.swakpak.com 1-866-SWAK-PAK

Eileen Tucker Cosby, Author

As an African American raised in Utah during the height of civil rights, Eileen has a personal interest in helping children and their families to embrace the differences in people. Eileen has been fortunate to experience the lifestyles of people from various backgrounds and is grateful for the positive influences that these experiences have made in her life. *"D" is for DIVERSITY* is Eileen's gift of love to people all over the world.

Eileen is an encouragement and empowerment expert. Her insightful vision of people lets her see what is possible for them in their lives and in business. She speaks to corporations and sales teams about the importance of a positive attitude to achieve and maintain established goals. Her inspiring presentations transfer valuable experience to increase personal and business success. For more information about her consulting services or speaking, call 480-557-6749 or email eileen@swakpak.com.

Norma S. Strange, Illustrator

Norma has always had a love for people. As a child being raised in Kentucky, she has always appreciated people for who they are and not their appearance. Norma has a natural interest in people and their different perspectives. She believes we all have a unique talent that is enlarged as we collaborate and work together to create solutions. Norma is excited to focus her graphic design and artistic talents on the message in *"D" is for DIVERSITY.* It is her hope that this book will open the doors of communication between parents and their children concerning the topic of diversity or better yet, unconditionally loving one another.

Norma, *The Marketing Magnifier*, consults with businesses to help them gain more from their current marketing efforts. She speaks to entrepreneurs of all ages teaching them to brand more effectively. Her inspiring presentations are humorous and jam-packed with successful business ideas. For more information about her consulting, services or speaking, call 480-557-6749 or email nstrange@swakpak.com.

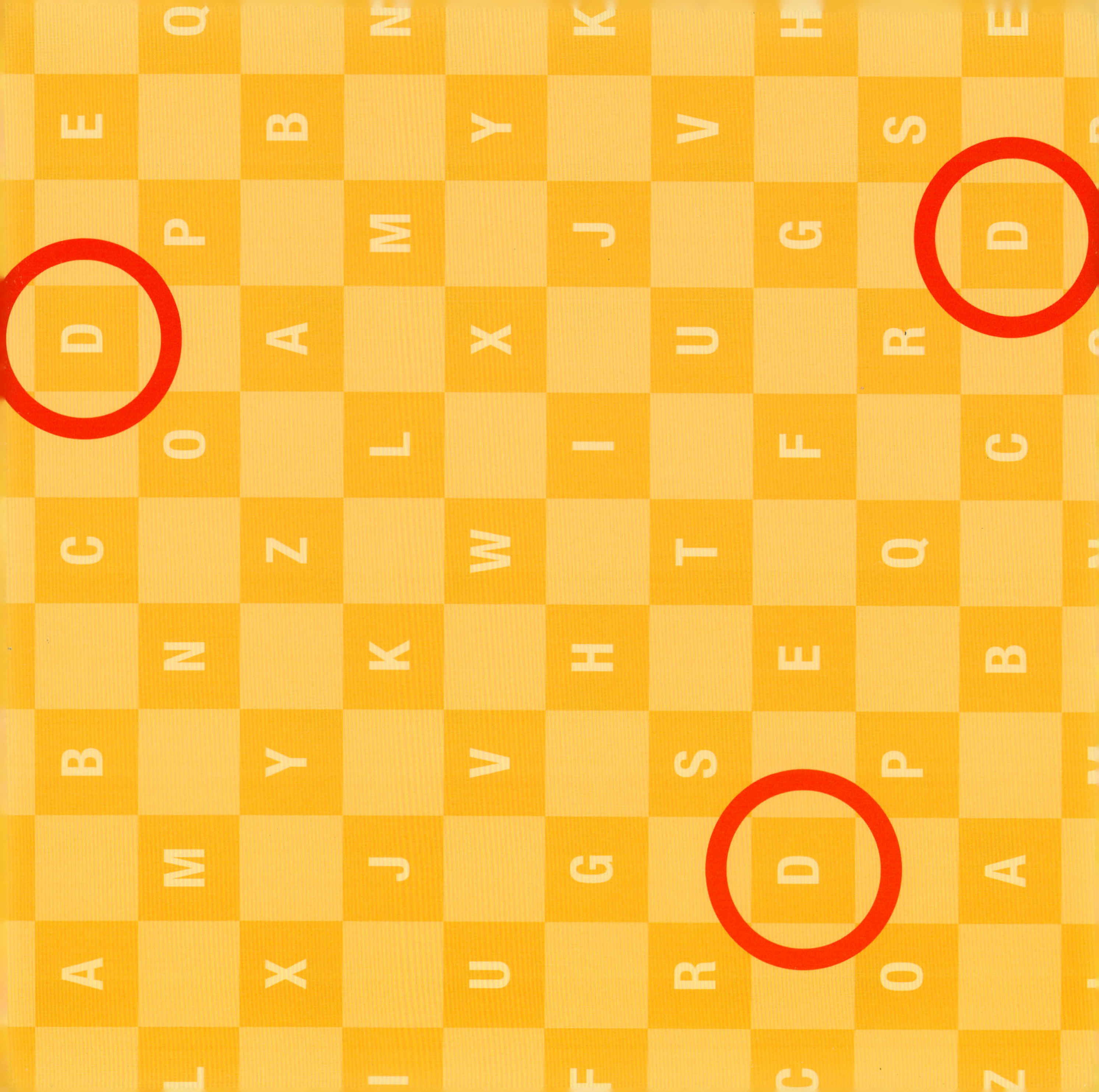